First Edition. 2021

LITTLE STAR LOST

Story by Davena O'Neill

Illustrations by Evelyn Vázquez

Little Star once fell from the night sky.

He missed being in the heavens,

and so, began to cry.

Rabbit while out hopping
was dazzled by the bright.
She went to investigate,
what had lit up the night.

She found Star crying,

and offered to assist.

“I’ll help get you home,

before you’re even missed”.

So, off they set together,
Star lighting the way,
anxious to get home
before the break of day.

"We'll head to the mountain,
it's close to heaven there".
But all at once, they heard a noise
that made them stop and stare.

It was a frightful howling,

Fox caught in a trap.

Little Star shone his beam,

and released him with a zap.

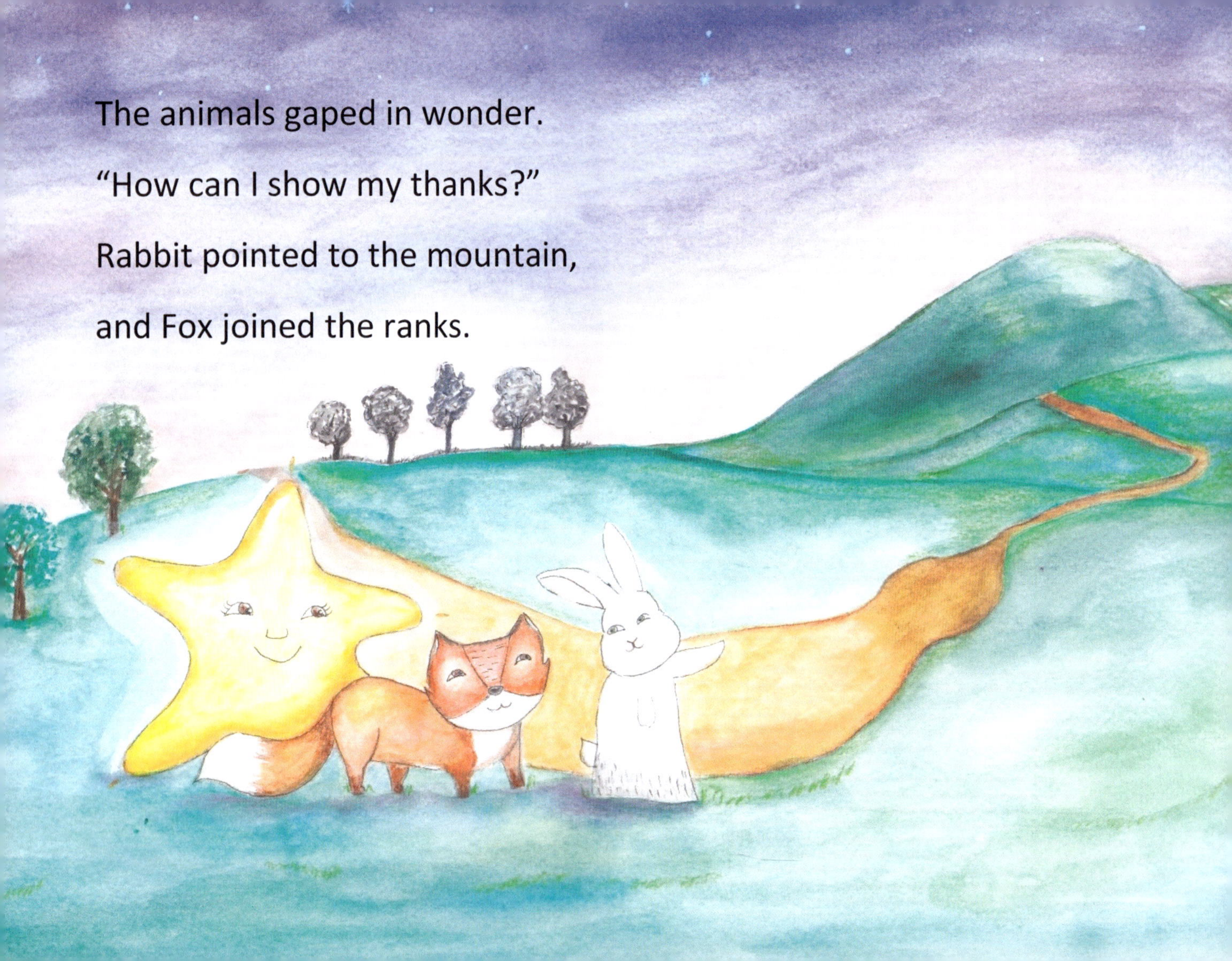

The animals gaped in wonder.

“How can I show my thanks?”

Rabbit pointed to the mountain,

and Fox joined the ranks.

Off the trio travelled,

a way home to find.

Unaware of the trail of stardust,

that was being left behind.

All at once a mighty crash,

made the three friends jump together.

Young Buck had tangled up his antlers in....

Moss...

Twigs...

And Heather.

Little Star stepped forward,

and shone his light directly.

Buck reared up, shook his head,

delighted to be free.

And so, now four took the mountain road,

climbing ever higher.

The trail of light grew longer,

and Star began to tire.

Suddenly before them,

a nest fell from a tree.

Little Star rose up,

and placed it safely among the leaves.

Mother Bird tweeted thanks

and watched the group move on.

As they neared the mountaintop,

they were blessed with her song.

But little Star had grown smaller still,
and had no strength remaining.
He could not reach up to the sky,
with all his stretch and straining.

The animals huddled close,

then stood one on the other.

Buck, then Fox, and Rabbit,

with Star on top of her.

Above, the Moon was watching,

she came as close as she could.

But little Star was still out of reach,

until a noise came from the woods.

A dozen birds came flying,

and took hold of little Star.

They rose into the night sky.

Now Moon was not so far.

Moon opened out her arms,

took Star in her embrace.

He cuddled up against her,

with a smile on his face.

“I saw your light from heaven,

all the kindness that you shared.

Even when it took your strength and size,

you still showed that you cared.”

The animals waved goodbye,

happy for their friend.

They followed his path back to their homes,

their adventure at an end.

Though his time was short among them,

he really made a mark.

And showed how acts of kindness

can be a light in the dark.

And while they will miss him,

they know they can always see

him shining in the night sky,

as happy as can be.

The End

For Daniel.

Shine bright little Star.

For Sarah.

DO'N

For Stephen & Lucia.

EV

Thanks to Ali and Dan for choosing this story as the winning entry to "A Story for Daniel" 2020.

Thanks to Evelyn for her beautiful illustrations, bringing this story to life.

Thanks to Martin O'Brien for putting it all together.

Thanks to family, friends and supporters. And thanks to all who have bought this book, raising funds for such a worthy cause.

Happy reading and sweet dreams.

Davena.

Daniel was a beautiful, bright and funny 21-month-old baby when he died of relapsed blood cancer. He loved animals, music, storybooks, watching telly and eating chocolate cake.

This book honours Daniel's memory so beautifully, please enjoy it as much as we did 😊

Dan and Ali Farbrace.

Profits from the sales of this book are going to raise money for the Daniel Farbrace Brighter Future Fund & Great Ormond Street Hospital.

Printed in Great Britain
by Amazon